rhyme

ounting rhyme activities

for early years

Jenni Tavener

Author
Jenni Tavener

Editor
Jane Bishop

Assistant editor
Sally Gray

Series designer
Joy White

Designer
Claire Belcher

Illustrations
Cathy Hughes

Cover
Sarah Laver

Designed using Aldus Pagemaker
Processed by Scholastic Ltd, Leamington Spa

Published by Scholastic Ltd, Villiers House, Clarendon Avenue,
Leamington Spa, Warwickshire CV32 5PR

For my parents Jack and Irene Yates

British Library Cataloguing-in-Publication Data
A catalogue record for this book is available from the British Library.
ISBN 0-590-53656-7

Contents

chapter four

One, two buckle my shoe

chapter five

One, two, three, four, five

photocopiable activities

Bun medley

Objective
Music – to work as a team to compose music for the rhyme.

Group size
Small or large groups.

What you need
A copy of the music for the rhyme (page 7), pictures and photographs of different foods and food shops, a local shopping parade (optional).

Preparation
Sing the rhyme and look at the pictures and photos of foods and food shops.

If possible, visit a local shopping parade with small groups of children to observe the variety of food shops.

What to do
Ask the children to use their observations of the different foods and food shops to create a new version of the rhyme. Ask them to decide what type of food they would like to sing about, perhaps chocolate cakes, juicy apples or fruit sweets.

Ask where they might be able to purchase their chosen food, for example juicy apples could come from a market stall. Next, ask the children to describe their chosen food, 'juicy apples' for example could be: 'shiny and red with a stalk on top'.

The children can then invent the cost of their chosen food and a 'customer' – it might be a girl, a friend, a policeman or a clown.

Put all the ideas together to create an interesting new rhyme:

'Five juicy apples
In a market stall
Shiny and red
With a stalk on top
Along came a policeman
With five pennies one day
Brought a juicy apple
And took it right away.'

Discussion
Throughout the activity encourage the children to share their ideas, to take turns and to listen to the views of other children.

For younger children
Encourage the children to use the original rhyme and just change one section: Five currant buns in a Baker's shop, Big and round with a *strawberry* on the top.

For older children
Encourage the children to work in pairs or small groups and invite each group to write their song down. Compile a 'song book' containing all the new songs that the children have written.

Follow-up activities
▲ Tape-record the children singing their new compositions.
▲ Create a picture sequence story about the new songs. Encourage older children to write some of the words.
▲ Make percussion instruments to play while singing the new songs.

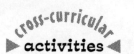

Carrying and collecting buns

Objective
PE – to play a game which reinforces co-operation and team work.

Group size
Up to four teams of up to six (an equal number in each team).

What you need
Each team will need a large PE hoop, a plastic or non shatter tray, one item of small PE apparatus for each child (ball, bean bag, quoit), sufficient space for the children to move around freely and safely.

Preparation
Place the large PE hoops on the floor in a line. Inside each hoop place the balls, bean bags and so on (one piece for each child). Explain that these represent 'buns' and 'cakes'. Help the children in each team to form a line approximately 15–20 paces away from their 'buns' and 'cakes'. Provide the first child in each team with an empty tray.

What to do
The first child in each team runs up to their hoop and places one 'bun' onto their tray. The child then runs back to the team and hands over the tray and 'bun' to the next player (if they drop their 'bun', they must stop to pick it up and replace it on their tray).

The second player in each team takes the tray and returns to the hoop to collect a second 'bun'. This player should then travel back to their team whilst making sure the two 'buns' remain on the tray. The tray plus 'buns' is then passed to the third team member. Play continues. The winners are the first team to remove all the 'buns' from their hoop.

Discussion
Ask the children if they can explain the rules of the game to you. Ask: what would happen if the tray was dropped? What would happen if the teams didn't have the same number of children?

For younger children
Ask the children to collect and carry only one 'bun' at a time.

For older children
Challenge the older children by providing only spherical objects to carry which will require them to carry the tray very evenly to avoid the 'buns' rolling off the tray.

Follow-up activities
▲ Invite the children to adapt the game using new ideas of their own.
▲ Encourage the children to write rules and instructions for their game.
▲ Use a wide range of materials such as pencils, pens, paints, fabric, card, coloured paper, foil, lace and tissue to create a collage based on their game.

▲ **18**
Starting with rhyme
Counting rhyme activities

A recipe for kindness

Objective
RE – to develop an awareness of kindness to others.

Group size
Small or large groups.

What you need
A comfortable place to sit, a sheet of A1 sized paper, pens and pencils.

Preparation
Draw a large red heart clearly on to the sheet of A1 paper.

What to do
Encourage the children to share views and ideas about 'being kind' by inviting them to talk about somebody who has been kind or caring to them. Ask the children to recall something kind, helpful or loving which this person has done.

Let the children take turns to write down their special memory inside the large heart (or scribe the words for them).

Add the caption 'A recipe for kindness' and mount on the wall to create a thought provoking display.

Discussion
Explain that a 'recipe for kindness' is a play on words. Refer back to the rhyme and explain to the children that a recipe for a currant bun includes all the different things needed to help make the bun, but in this activity they are writing a 'recipe for kindness'. Ask who helps you when you are sad? Who is kind to you when you need a friend?

For younger children
Invite them to draw a picture of their special memory or a kind person.

For older children
Invite the children to draw or cut out a small heart to write in. Help them to write the caption – 'A recipe for love' on one side and to list all the ingredients which make someone loving on the other side. Thread all the hearts together to create an interesting mobile.

Follow-up activities
▲ Write a 'thank you' card or letter to someone who has been kind.
▲ Make heart-shaped biscuits to share with friends and relatives.

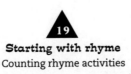

Tea party

Informative writing.

Picture sequence - how the buns were made.

Interactive questions.

Cooking Currant Buns

We made

Our tea

Printed or painted 'currant' border.

Ingredients used to bake the buns.

Can — ?

How = ?

How ——— ?

Pasta Recipes

Children's cooking

Our Recipe File

My favourite recipe

Recipes written by the children and stored in a book.

Group size
Small groups.

What you need
Recipe and ingredients to make currant buns (see page 22), display board, low table, a sealed bag of flour, sealed bag of sugar, empty margarine tub, an egg, a salt pot, sealed packet of dried yeast, a sealed packet/box of currants (alternatively place a small amount of each ingredient into separate plastic tubs with transparent lids), a large tablecloth, cookery books, pens, pencils, paper, card, black paint, small sponge, shallow tray for printing, wool or ribbon.

Preparation
Make currant buns with the children, hold a simple tea party so the children can eat their buns and have a drink. Ask the children to write and draw about their experiences – 'How I made my buns', 'Our tea party', 'How I helped to wash up', 'Our recipe' and so on.

What to do
Help the children to set up an information display about their cooking experience.

Invite the children to draw a picture of a currant bun and to place it on the display board just above the sample ingredients. Attach ribbon or wool between the ingredients and picture to highlight the link between the raw and cooked product. Help the children to print a 'currant' border for their display using narrow strips of paper, a small sponge and black paint. Label the ingredients and include interactive labels to promote discussion. Display examples of the children's writing and drawings.

Discussion
Look at the interactive labels with the children asking: How many ingredients did you use? Which type of flour did you use? Can you find other cake recipes? Ask the children to think of questions for their display.

Follow-up activities
▲ Use recipe books to try out some other cake recipes.
▲ Collect favourite recipes from parents, grandparents and other visitors.
▲ Read the traditional story, *The gingerbread man* (Ladybird).

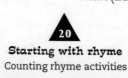

Thought for the day

Objective
RE – to explore the theme of saying 'thank you'.

Group size
Small groups.

What you need
Coloured pens and pencils, drawing paper, drafting paper.

Preparation
Say the rhyme together and tell the children that some people say a prayer at bedtime. Ask them whether they do. Remind them about 'prayers' by talking about the prayers which the children have heard during recent assemblies or while at their local church, mosque or other place of worship.

Explain that some prayers are to give thanks to God for things that have happened to us or to people around us. (Be aware of the different religions of the children in your group and be sympathetic to the different interpretations of the word 'God' and to different styles of praying.)

What to do
Ask the children to recall a personal experience or general observation which they can be thankful for and invite them to draft their own prayer giving thanks. Suggest that they begin by writing 'Thank you God for ... a happy day/a special friend/beautiful flowers and so on.

When they are happy with their prayer encourage the children to copy it out tidily on a clean sheet of paper and to decorate the prayer with relevant pictures or a pattern around the border.

Discussion
Ask the children to explain what their prayer is about. Ask, when do people usually say their prayers? Why do we say prayers?

For younger children
Let the children work together in a small group and all contribute ideas towards one shared prayer. Scribe the words for them and then let them illustrate the sheet.

For older children
Invite the children to secure their individual prayers into a blank book to create a prayer book to share.

Follow-up activities
▲ Invite the children to read their prayers during assemblies or group sharing times.
▲ Display the children's prayers alongside their 'Thank you' paintings and drawings.
▲ Visit a local church, mosque or other religious centre. Arrange for someone to talk to the children about prayer time or other important rituals.

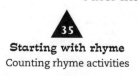

Teddies in bed

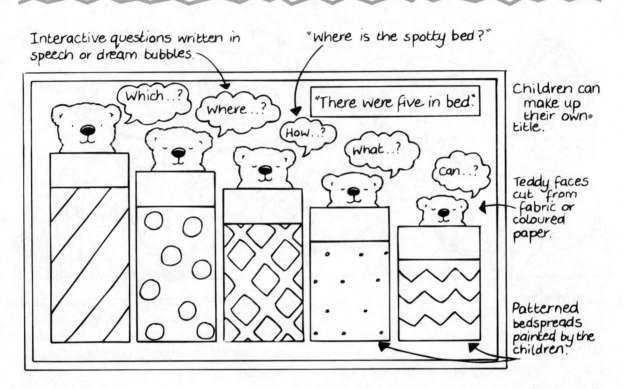

Interactive questions written in speech or dream bubbles.

"Where is the spotty bed?"

Which..?

Where..?

How..?

What..?

Can..?

"There were five in bed."

Children can make up their own title.

Teddy faces cut from fabric or coloured paper.

Patterned bedspreads painted by the children.

Group size
Small groups.

What you need
Paper, paints, painting equipment, fur or felt fabric, thick black permanent marker pen.

Preparation
Provide five (or ten) sheets of paper in different sizes.

What to do
Invite the children to paint each piece of paper with a different pattern to create a 'bedspread'. Help the children to cut out teddy bear heads in different sizes from paper, card or fabric. Let them draw in the teddy bears features using a thick black pen. Make sure the heads are an appropriate size for the 'bedspreads'.

Arrange the patterned bedspreads in size order across a display board. Position the teddy bear heads so that it appears that the teddy bears are in bed. Add a 'speech bubble' or 'dream cloud' next to each teddy bear.

Write interactive questions about the patterned bedspreads inside each bubble/cloud. Alternatively scribe questions devised by the children during discussion.

Discussion
Ask the children to describe the patterned bedspreads. Invite them to think of questions about the different patterns. Ask them to begin their question with words such as 'which', 'what', 'where' and 'how'. For example, they could ask: How many different patterns can you see? Where is the spotty bed? Can you find the biggest bed? What do you think of that pattern?

Follow-up activities
▲ Invite the children to invent a title for their display.
▲ Use the display board to inspire mathematical language such as bigger than, smaller than, biggest, how wide?, wider and longest.
▲ Use the display to increase awareness of 'which', 'when' and 'how'.

Memory quilt

Group size
Small groups.

What you need
Fabric, sewing needles and thread, *The Patchwork Quilt* by Valerie Flournoy (Picture Puffin), paper, card, pens and pencils.

Preparation
Read the story *The Patchwork Quilt* to the children, which is about a girl and her grandmother who sew a patchwork quilt. Each piece of fabric holds a special memory. Ask the children to each bring in a piece of fabric which holds a special memory (provide some samples for children who are unable to bring in their own fabric). Cut the fabric into 20cm squares.

What to do
Help the children to sew the squares together. Twenty five individual squares of fabric will produce a 'patchwork quilt' of approximately one metre squared. When complete use a sewing machine to hem the raw edges of the quilt. Hang the quilt across a corner for an interesting display. Pin up written work and drawings completed by the children during the follow-up sessions around the quilt.

Discussion
If the children were able to bring in their own piece of fabric ask questions such as: what is your special memory? What did the fabric belong to? Let children who were unable to bring in their own piece of fabric explain why they chose a particular piece from the samples provided.

Follow-up activities
▲ Encourage the children to glue a sample of their piece of fabric onto a sheet of card or paper and then write about their special memories.
▲ Write a joint book review of *The Patchwork Quilt* with everyone contributing a page.
▲ Create detailed drawings or paintings of the finished quilt.

Close observational drawing of quilt.

Colourful border.

Descriptive work about quilt.

Book review of "The Patchwork Quilt".

Child sewn "memory quilt".

Corner display board (or corner of wall).

Children's written work.

The story book.

A book or folder of children's written work.

Milkshake bedtime drink

Group size
Three children.

What you need
Ingredients for three drinks: a pint of milk, 100g of soft fresh fruit (strawberries, raspberries, banana) or tinned fruit (apricots, pineapple) chocolate flake, caster sugar, a scoop of vanilla ice cream (optional). Utensils: a blender or hand whisk, fork, plastic bowl, ½ pint plastic tumblers, straws.

Preparation
Wash hands and put on a clean apron. Place the peeled and chopped fruit in a bowl and mash it with a fork.

What to do
Place the mashed fruit, milk, sugar and ice cream into a blender and mix for 30 seconds.

If you do not have a blender, mix with a whisk or fork. Pour into two tumblers. Sprinkle flaked chocolate on top. Drink with a straw immediately.

Discussion
Ask the children to recall the ingredients and sequence of events. Ask them: how many grams of fruit did you use? How did you mix the ingredients together? What did you do to the fruit first?

Follow-up activities
▲ Encourage the children to wash up the utensils and clean the surfaces.
▲ Talk about other favourite drinks which the children could help to make, such as orange squash.
▲ Invite the children to write or draw about their milkshake recipe.

▲ 38
Starting with rhyme
Counting rhyme activities

A meeting point

Objective
RE – to develop an empathy for the feelings of others when lost or lonely.

Group size
Small or large groups.

What you need
A copy of the rhyme, a large outdoor plant container (wood, plastic or terracotta), soil, fertiliser, a dwarf evergreen plant, a packet of flower seeds (or bedding plants), a spare area outside.

Preparation
Say the rhyme with the children, and talk about where the lost ducks might have gone. How did they find their mother? Ask the children if they have ever been lost? How were they found?

What to do
Invite the children to help create a plant and flower display to use as a meeting point for children who get lost from their friends at your school, nursery or playgroup. Take the children on to the playground to look for a suitable place for their meeting point.

When you have selected an appropriate location, help the children to position their container and to plant their evergreen and seeds or bedding plants.

Invite the children to paint or stencil the words 'meeting point' using exterior paint on their container.

Discussion
Talk about how the children feel when they are lost or lonely. Ask questions such as: how can you help someone who is lost or lonely in the playground? Discuss what it feels like to be without a friend to play with. Ask questions such as: how can you help someone who has no one to play with?

For younger children
Invite the children to create a pictorial record of how they set up their 'meeting point'.

For older children
Encourage the children to create a written record of how they set up their 'meeting point', illustrating it if they wish.

Follow-up activities
▲ Care for the 'meeting point' flower display by watering, weeding and planting new flowers or seeds.
▲ Refer back to the rhyme and invite the children to write an account or draw a picture about where they think the 'lost' ducks disappeared to, and how they were eventually found.
▲ Take photographs of the 'meeting point' in use, display the photographs in a prominent place to inform visitors or 'new-comers' about the resource.

Feathers

Group size
Small groups.

What you need
One or more hats with a decorative feather (or pictures of such hats), a collection of real feathers, paper, card, cereal boxes, sticky tape, strong adhesive, pictures/photographs of birds, objects made using feathers such as a feather duster and quill pen, drawing media, roll of corrugated paper (optional).

Preparation
Check that none of the children are allergic to feathers. Invite the children to look at the pictures of the birds to observe the different feathers. Show the children the hats and objects which have feathers on/in them.

Ask the children to design and make their own hat with a feather decoration. Use real feathers or cut out feather shapes from coloured paper and snip the edges to create a fringe or feathery effect.

What to do
Use a roll of corrugated card to back the display. Cover some tubs and buckets with plain fabric and position them on a display block in front. Place the hats at different heights on the boxes. Pin up the children's work on to the background. Add interactive questions to the display, such as: how many hats can you see? When would you wear this hat?

Place the objects and artefacts made using feathers in the display for the children to observe and handle.

Discussion
Ask questions to stimulate an interest in the display and to increase curiosity about feathers. Ask: are feathers light or heavy? What colour can a feather be? What happens if a feather gets wet?

Follow-up activities
▲ Use a variety of media to create observational pictures of feathers.
▲ Write or draw using a quill pen.
▲ Mount real feathers on card and label them with the name of the bird that it belonged to.
▲ Use information books to find out about different birds and their types of feathers.
▲ Time how long it takes for different feathers to reach the ground.

Child's picture of feathers.

Photographs or posters of birds.

Interactive questions.

Corrugated card.

A display of objects made using feathers.

Hats - some made by the children, some commercial.

Real feather collage.

Children's quill pen writing or patterns.

Real feathers labelled with the bird's name - 'A Budgie feather'.

Hook-a-duck game

Children's collage or painted background.

Green card cut like blades of grass.

Low table draped in a green cloth.

Six plastic ducks with fabric loops.

Shiny blue or silver foil pond.

Interactive labels

Hook a Duck game

What is your highest score?

What is your lowest score?

How ___ ?

Our Rules and

Bucket or box containing two rods.

Group size
Small groups.

What you need
A low table, a drape, (various shades of green), green card, scissors, two dowelling rods, small box/bucket, shiny blue paper (or foil), six identical plastic ducks, paper, paints and brushes, aprons, stapler, sticky labels, sticky tape, six strips of non fraying fabric (15cm × 2cm) folded to create a loop.

Preparation
Cover a low table in a green drape. Let the children help to cut several strips of green card to resemble thick blades of grass, attach these to the edges of the table. Invite the children to cut a large 'duck pond' from shiny paper. Put in the centre of the table.

Ask the children to paint a background scene showing 'hills far away'. Mount the scenery onto a display board or wall behind the table. Attach a loop of fabric to the back of the six ducks using strong sticky tape.

What to do
Ask the children to help make the 'hook a duck' game. Place a number label on to the base of the six plastic ducks (vary the numbers to suit your group). Encourage the children to use the interactive display to play the following games:

Game 1: Take turns to hook up two or more ducks using the rods. Add the score. Replace the ducks. The highest score wins. Play again, but this time the lowest score wins.

Game 2: Hook two ducks. Take the lowest number away from the highest number. The winner is the player with the highest score.

Discussion
Ask questions such as: what is your highest score? How many ducks do you need to 'hook up' to get a score of more than 3? Can you make up a new game? Tell me the rules of your new game.

Follow-up activities
▲ Invite the children to write the rules and instructions for the games.
▲ Add five cardboard or plastic fish to the 'pond', attach a fabric loop to the top of each fish and 'plus' or 'minus' signs to the underside of each fish. Use the game to help the children develop an understanding of mathematical symbols.

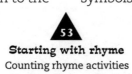

Duck face mini pizzas

Group size
Up to four children.

What you need
For four pizza's: two soft wholemeal baps – halved, four tablespoons of pizza topping, 100g grated cheese, eight frozen peas, an orange pepper. Grill, four plastic plates, tablespoon, vegetable knife (to be used by adults only).

Preparation
Wash hands, put a clean apron on.

What to do
Lightly toast both sides of the four bap halves. Spread one tablespoon of pizza topping over each bap half, and sprinkle 25g of grated cheese onto each bap half.

Decorate by using two peas on each pizza to make eyes. Cut the orange pepper into eight strips and place two strips onto each pizza to create the ducks beak.

Place the pizzas under the grill until the cheese melts.

Discussion
Ask questions to encourage an awareness of health and safety while cooking: Why do we need to wash our hands before cooking? Why do knives need to be handled carefully? Why must we be careful when using a grill?

Follow-up activities
▲ Encourage the children to wash up and dry their own plates.
▲ Make animal face pizzas using a range of different shaped vegetable slices such as mushrooms which make good ears or noses, spring onion shreds which made good whiskers and cucumber slices for eyes.
▲ Make a health and safety cookery poster.

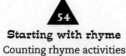

Sound around

Objective
Music – to inspire an appreciation of sound and to develop listening skills.

Group size
Small or large groups.

What you need
A cassette recorder and cassette, a comfortable place to sit.

Preparation
Record a series of five everyday sounds. If possible link some of the sounds to the themes in the rhyme, for example shoes tapping, a door shutting, sticks breaking, a gate creaking and a hen clucking.

What to do
Invite the children to sit in a comfortable quiet area. Play the prepared cassette to them and encourage them to listen carefully to each sound and to identify what they hear. If necessary you could provide simple clues to help or invite them to ask you questions.

When the sounds have all been identified divide the children into two groups. Help each group in turn to record five new sounds for the other group to identify.

Discussion
Talk about the different sounds. Encourage the children to think of their own descriptions and to explain where or when they might hear each sound. Talk about the variety of sounds around such as helpful sounds like a car horn to warn us of danger or a bell to tell us when playtime is over, happy sounds such as laughing, clapping, jolly music, or mechanical sounds such as a lawn mower, a tractor, a pneumatic drill and so on.

For younger children
Begin by offering visual clues such as pictures to help the children identify the sounds. As the children's listening skills develop encourage them to rely on the sound alone.

For older children
Record sounds which require more detailed listening skills. For example, a door opening compared to a door shutting or feet walking compared to jumping or tapping.

Follow-up activities
▲ Use percussion instruments to record different sounds.
▲ Accompany the children on a sound walk – listen for traffic, birds, aeroplanes and other vehicles.
▲ Listen to a variety of music including classical, pop, jazz and instrumental, to develop a sense of musical appreciation and knowledge of the variety available.

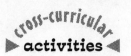

Dancing shoes

Objective
PE – to act out a dance in response to instructions.

Group size
Any size.

What you need
A room with enough space for the children to move around freely and safely, a pair of tap, or dancing slippers or shoes, a recording of some cheerful instrumental music.

Preparation
Show the dancing shoes or slippers to the children. Stimulate their imagination by creating a story entitled 'The Dancing Shoes'. Adapt and extend this idea with the children's own ideas: Once upon a time a child was walking in the park when he/she saw a pair of shoes lying on the grass. 'That is a funny place to leave a pair of shoes,' the boy thought. Then he noticed a label attached to them, it read 'put me on'. 'I must not put them on, they are not mine,' thought the boy. But he was very curious and so he did. 'I'll just put them on quickly then I'll take them off and leave them where I found them for the owner to collect,' thought the boy.

So the boy tried the shoes on. Something very strange began to happen. One foot started to tap. Then the other foot began to tap. Then both feet began to tap and before long the boy was dancing around the park.

He tried to stop but he couldn't, the shoes were stuck on his feet and they would not stop dancing.

What to do
Invite the children to re-enact the scenes from this story. Let them begin by each miming the child putting the magic shoes on, then tapping one foot, then the other foot, then both feet. Encourage the children to make up their own dance as they move around the room.

Then continue the story with the children's ideas – include jumps, hops, twists and skips. Encourage the children to create a short, simple dance of, say three or four movements – for example a twist, a jump and two leaps in the air.

End the activity by explaining that the child had danced all the way home: 'He/she was so tired that he/she fell fast asleep and the shoes danced all the way back to the park on their own.'

Tell the children to finish their dance by lying down, still and quiet.

Discussion
Ask the children some questions to stimulate their memory: where did the child find the shoes? What dances or movements did the boy do? What happened when the boy got home?

For younger children
Simplify the movements and show the children what to do.

For older children
Use the children's ideas to adapt the story.

Follow-up activities
▲ Invite the children to retell the story in words, pictures or in writing.
▲ Let the children use paints, pastels, chalks or crayons to make a drawing of the shoes shown to them.

I can...

Objective
RE – to develop confidence and self-esteem, and to value each other's achievements.

Group size
Small and large groups.

What you need
A comfortable place to sit, the shoes the children are wearing.

Preparation
Say the rhyme together and encourage the children to think of something which they can do with their own shoes. They may suggest: fasten the buckle, do up the laces, put them on, jump in them, run fast in them, tap their feet quietly or loudly. Find something positive that every child can do! Then invite the children to try out their skills.

What to do
Invite the children to sit in a circle, making sure that each child is comfortable and that they can see easily. Join in the circle yourself. Encourage the children to take it in turns to say and show the rest of the group what they can do with or in their shoes. (Make sure that it is safe for them to do so.)

Ask the children to begin by saying their name, followed by 'I can...', for example 'I am Joe and I can jump in my shoes'.

Joe should then jump up and down to show everybody what he can do. Encourage the rest of the group to show Joe that he has done well by clapping or by saying 'well done'.

Discussion
Ask questions to show that you are interested in each child's achievement and that you value their skill: how long did it take you to learn that? When did you learn? How often do you have to practise? Encourage the children to ask each other similar questions.

For younger children
Provide extra reassurance by moving and standing next to the children who may be shy about talking in front of others or who need encouragement to show their achievement.

For older children
Some children might enjoy learning a new skill especially to show everyone. Help them during the preparation session to decide what they wish to learn and to ensure that it is an achievable and safe aim!

Follow-up activities
▲ Record the children's personal achievements in words or pictures. Secure work in a book or folder entitled 'I can...'.
▲ Take photographs of each child during the 'circle time' while they are demonstrating their achievement. Display the photographs in a prominent position. Title the display 'We can...'.

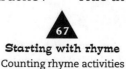

Boots and shoes

Group size
Small groups.

What you need
A wide selection of clean boots and shoes (such as football boots, wellington boots, baby booties, roller-blades, children's shoes, slippers, ice-skates, ballet shoes, hockey boots, sandals, flippers, clogs and so on). Stories and rhymes about boots or shoes – *The slipper and the rose, Cinderella, Puss in boots, The elves and the shoemaker, There was an old woman who lived in a shoe* (all traditional tales), photographs of the children wearing a pair of favourite shoes. Paints, paper, shallow tray for printing, display boxes, drapes.

Preparation
Create a 'stimulus display' by arranging the wide variety of boots and shoes on a table at the children's own height. Add interest to the display by arranging the shoes and boots on boxes of different heights. Include in the display a range of story and rhyme books about boots and shoes. If possible ask the children to bring in photographs of them wearing a special or favourite pair of shoes.

What to do
Use the stimulus display to attract the children's interest and attention and to inspire them to observe and discuss the items on show. Invite them to draw and write about the boots and shoes and use this work to transform the stimulus display into a display of children's work.

Discussion
Ask questions to develop a greater awareness about the different functions of the shoes and boots on display: Who would wear booties? When do you wear wellington boots? Why would flippers be worn? Invite the children to think of their own questions. Write them down and use them as interactive labels for the display.

Follow-up activities
▲ Invite the children to write a description of the shoes.
▲ Create a border of sole or foot prints.
▲ Inspire the children to write their own stories about boots and shoes. Use published stories (or the activity 'The Magic Buckle' on page 56) to stimulate ideas.

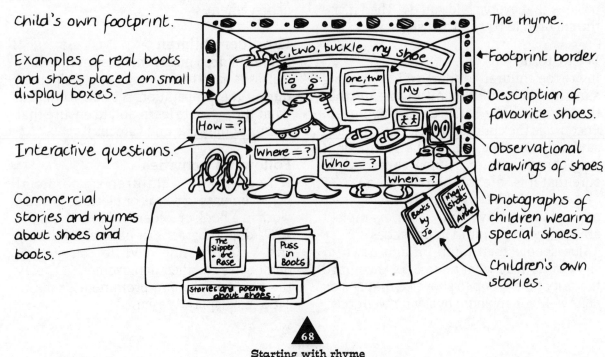

Child's own footprint.

Examples of real boots and shoes placed on small display boxes.

Interactive questions.

Commercial stories and rhymes about shoes and boots.

The rhyme.

Footprint border.

Description of favourite shoes.

Observational drawings of shoes.

Photographs of children wearing special shoes.

Children's own stories.

One, two, buckle my shoe.

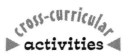
Fishy instruments

Objective
Music – to find out how different sounds and instruments can be made.

Group size
Individuals or small groups.

What you need
Percussion instruments, bells, dowelling, strong tape, beads, lentils, rice, buttons, fabric, coloured paper, shiny paper, card, plastic bottles, yoghurt pots, kitchen roll tubes, tubs, wool, scissors, felt-tipped pens, pictures of fish and sea creatures.

Preparation
Sing the rhyme together and encourage the children to use the percussion instruments to accompany the singing. Use books and pictures to find out about different types of fish and creatures which live in the sea.

What to do
Invite the children to design and make their own musical instruments on the theme of fish or sea creatures. Here are some ideas:

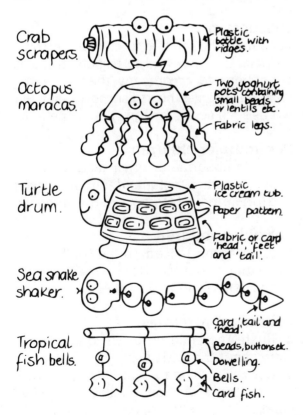

Crab scrapers: Attach card 'claws' and 'eyes' to a plastic bottle with ridges. Rub objects along the ridges to make different sounds.

Octopus maracas: Attach eight fabric 'legs' and 'eyes' to a kitchen roll tube sealed at both ends or seal two yoghurt pots together. Place small objects inside the containers to make different sounds.

Turtle drum: Attach a card 'head', 'feet' and 'tail' to a round ice cream or margarine tub. Decorate the sides with brown squares or coloured paper.

Sea snake shaker: Thread coloured beads, buttons or other objects onto wool or string. Attach a card 'face' to one end and card 'tail' to the other.

Tropical fish bells: Tape or tie three or four lengths of wool to a piece of dowelling or an old pencil. Attach some bells and small colourful 'fish' cut from card, fabric or shiny paper.

Discussion
Sing the rhyme together and ask the children to recall other songs and rhymes about fish or fishing. When they are creating their creatures encourage the children to tell you what their creatures will look and sound like.

For younger children
Make a simple imaginary sea creature using a tub drum, bottle scraper or yoghurt pot maracas and so on.

For older children
Emphasise the 'design' stage by inviting the children to begin by sketching some ideas and experimenting with different sounds before tackling the 'make' stage.

Follow-up activities
▲ Use the instruments to compose simple tunes and write songs about the sea and its mysterious creatures.
▲ Invite the children to use their instruments to accompany them while they sing songs about fish and fishing.

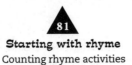

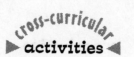

Swim little fishy

Objective
PE – to follow instructions and perform an expressive mime or dance.

Group size
Whole group.

What you need
Space for children to move around freely and safely.

Preparation
Make up a story about a little fish and incorporate opportunities for the children to act out the part of the fish by improvising its movements and antics.

What to do
Adapt and extend the following story to suit your children:

There was a little fish who lived in a quiet stream. He was bored of swimming up and down all day and wanted to have an adventure. (The children pretend to be the fish swimming up and down.) He decided to swim off and find the sea. Boats rushed past and made the little fish spin round and round in the water. (The children 'spin' like little fish.)

When the little fish saw the fishing nets and other obstacles he had to swim carefully in and out of them. (The children weave from side to side to avoid the imaginary hooks.)

The enormous waves in the sea made the little fish crash up and down. (The children mime crashing up and down.) A whale swam towards the fish, but the fish swam away until it came to a dark underwater cave. (The children mime swimming away from the whale and pretend to be feeling their way in a dark underwater cave.)

The little fish swam towards a chink of light at the end of the cave and to his amazement he found that he had swum all the way back to his little stream. He jumped in and out of the water with joy. (Let the children jump up and down pretending to be the little fish jumping for joy.)

Complete the session by inviting the children to make up a little dance to show how happy the little fish was.

Discussion
Encourage the children to suggest their own ideas for the story, and corresponding ideas for actions to accompany them. Ask the children to suggest how a fish moves – suggest words such as slither and glide to them.

For younger children
Use a tambourine or other instrument to help signal when to stop and start the actions and to help indicate fast or slow movements.

For older children
Emphasise the dance at the end of the story by inviting the children to create a sequence dance to perform to the other children.

Follow-up activities
▲ Invite the children to write or draw a story about the 'little fish'.
▲ Use the session to stimulate ideas for a 'comic strip' story about a little fish. Older children can include speech bubbles.

Caring for animals

Objective
RE – to increase awareness about caring for animals.

Group size
Small groups.

What you need
White A4 paper, coloured paper, (optional – a pet animal and owner to visit), stapler, coloured pens or pencils, thin white card (10cm squared).

Preparation
If possible arrange for a pet and its owner to visit the children to talk about its needs and how it is cared for. Make a four page 'pocket' booklet for each child using four sheets of white A4 paper (see below). Fold and staple together and add a cover using a sheet of coloured paper or card.

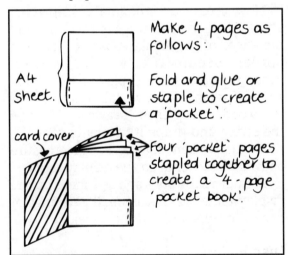

Make 4 pages as follows:

Fold and glue or staple to create a 'pocket'.

Four 'pocket' pages stapled together to create a '4-page 'pocket book'.

What to do
Ask each child to draw either their own pet (if they have one) or the visiting class pet on to a sheet of card. Encourage them to each think of four things which the pet needs to help keep it safe, healthy and comfortable – for example, a pet dog might require dog food, a basket, a park to exercise and a bone to chew.

Invite the children to draw a picture and write about each 'need' one on each of the four pages in their 'pocket' booklet. When complete, the children can place their 'pet' into the appropriate pocket on the page as they read about the needs of their pet.

Discussion
Refer back to the rhyme. Share views about how the children can help take care of animals in the wild. Discuss the different habitats of these creatures and talk about why we should help to keep local ponds, rivers, streams, parks and hedgerows clean and rubbish free.

For younger children
Scribe the words for the children or help each child to complete one page and then compile all the work into one large book for everyone to share.

For older children
Invite the children to create a book about four different animals. Draw four animals onto four small sheets of card, and then draw and write about all the needs of each animal onto the four separate pages in their pocket booklet. The children can then match the correct animal to the correct page as they read about the needs of each pet.

Follow-up activities
▲ Encourage the children to read their books out loud as a stimulus for further discussion about how to care for different animals.
▲ Arrange to keep a small pet (a goldfish or a hamster) in your group. Organise a rota so that everyone joins in taking care and responsibility for its welfare.

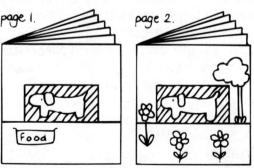

Picture of pet can be removed and placed into different 'pockets' as child reads booklet.

An underwater shipwreck

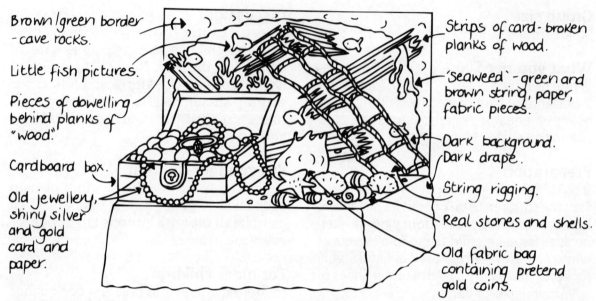

Brown/green border - cave rocks.

Little fish pictures.

Pieces of dowelling behind planks of "wood".

Cardboard box.

Old jewellery, shiny silver and gold card and paper.

Strips of card - broken planks of wood.

'seaweed' - green and brown string, paper, fabric pieces.

Dark background. Dark drape.

String rigging.

Real stones and shells.

Old fabric bag containing pretend gold coins.

Group size
Small groups.

What you need
Paints and painting equipment, black paper, green and brown string/strips of fabric, dark drape, string, dowelling or wood scraps, unwanted jewellery, box, shiny paper, play money, colourful beads, pictures/books about shipwrecks and underwater scenes, children's paintings or pictures of small fish, real shells and stones, gold and silver paper.

Preparation
Cover a display board in black paper and a table in a dark drape. Ask the children to make paintings of rocks/strips of wood using shades of grey, green and brown. Turn a cardboard box into a treasure chest using brown paint or sticky paper. Ask the children to cut pretend coins or jewellery from silver and gold paper. Thread beads to create necklaces and bracelets.

What to do
Look together at the pictures and books about shipwrecks and talk about some of the treasure that may have been lost.

Now create an imaginary shipwreck scene. Place the paintings of rocks around the edges of the display board to create a border. Secure the 'wooden planks' randomly across the display board. Drape strips of green and brown fabric/string over the wood to represent seaweed. Unravel the string and drape it unevenly over the scene to represent rigging. Put the treasure chest and contents on the display table.

Include real stones and sea shells on the display table and place small paintings of fish swimming around the wreck.

Discussion
Talk about the different types of life seen in the sea. Ask the children to tell you what treasures they would find and to describe them to you.

Follow-up activities
▲ Use the display to inspire imaginative stories and role-play activities about treasure ships and shipwrecks. Use spotted hankerchiefs and other dressing-up clothes to go with the stories.
▲ Invite the children to find out about some real shipwrecks such as the Mary Rose or the Titanic.

Bright fish

Group size
Small or large groups.

What you need
A tank of tropical fish (optional), dark blue background paper, brightly coloured border paper, shiny paper or foil, bright luminous paints, painting equipment, paper, pictures/photographs and picture books showing tropical fish or other brightly coloured fish.

Preparation
Cover a display board in dark blue background paper, add a wavy border cut from brightly coloured paper. Cut thin strands of shiny paper ready for use.

What to do
Invite the children to look at the tropical fish in the tank or in the pictures.

Ask the children to design and paint pictures of imaginary fish and seaweed. Cut them out and attach them to the display.

Place scrunched up paper behind the larger fish to give a three-dimensional effect. Secure the smaller fish to the display by using short strips of zigzagged paper like springs. The fish will move in the breeze.

Twist some strips of shiny paper and secure at the top and bottom of the display. These will move in the breeze to create a shimmering effect.

Discussion
Ask the children to describe the painted fish. Talk about the shapes, patterns and colours. Compare these fish with the real fish in the tank or the pictures of real fish.

Follow-up activities
▲ Encourage the children to write descriptions of the fish they have painted.
▲ Use the display to inspire mathematical language – which fish is the longest, shortest, widest, narrowest, thinnest and so on.
▲ Discuss how some fish change colour.

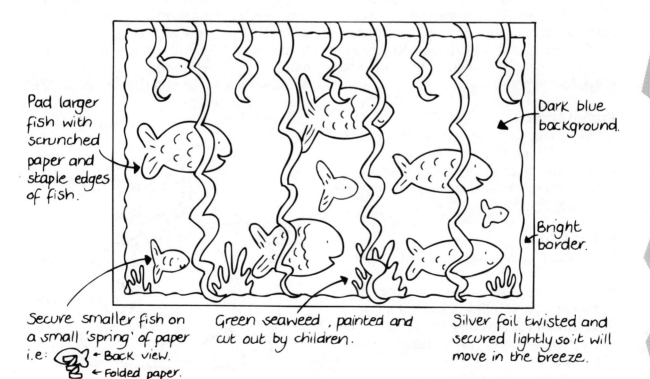

Pad larger fish with scrunched paper and staple edges of fish.

Dark blue background.

Bright border.

Secure smaller fish on a small 'spring' of paper i.e: ← Back view. ← Folded paper.

Green seaweed, painted and cut out by children.

Silver foil twisted and secured lightly so it will move in the breeze.